THE ULTIMATE
BALTIMORE RAVENS
TRIVIA BOOK

A Collection of Amazing Trivia Quizzes
and Fun Facts for Die-Hard Ravens Fans!

Ray Walker

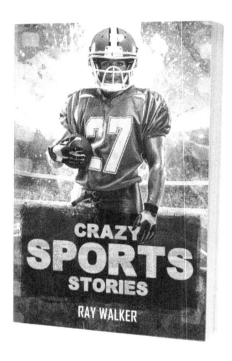

CONTENTS

INTRODUCTION

Team fandom should be inspirational. Our attachment to our favorite teams should fill us with pride, excitement, loyalty, and a sense of fulfillment in knowing that we are part of a community with many other fans who feel the same way.

Baltimore Ravens fans are no exceptions. With a rich, successful history in the NFL, the Ravens have inspired their supporters to strive for greatness with their tradition of colorful players, memorable eras, big moves, and unique moments.

This book is meant to be a celebration of those moments, and an examination of the collection of interesting, impressive, or important details that allow us to understand the full stories behind the players and the team.

You may use the book as you wish. Each chapter contains 20 quiz questions in a mixture of multiple choice and true or false formats, with an answer key (don't worry, it's on a separate page!) and a section of ten "Did You Know" factoids about the team.

Some will use it to test themselves with the quiz questions. How much Baltimore history did you really know? How many of the finer points can you remember? Some will use it competitively (isn't that the heart of sports?), waging contests with friends and fellow devotees to see who can lay claim to being the biggest fan. Some will enjoy it as a learning experience, gaining insight to enrich their fandom and add color to their understanding of their favorite team. Still others may use it to teach, sharing the wonderful anecdotes inside to inspire a new generation of fans to hop aboard the Ravens bandwagon.

Whatever your purpose may be, we hope you enjoy delving into the amazing background of Baltimore Ravens football!

Oh, for the record, information and statistics in this book are current up to the beginning of 2020. The Ravens will surely topple more records and win more awards as the seasons pass, so keep this in mind when you're watching the next game with your friends, and someone starts a conversation with "Did you know...."

CHAPTER 1:

ORIGINS & HISTORY

QUIZ TIME!

1. In which year did the Baltimore Ravens begin playing in the National Football League after being granted an expansion team?

   a. 1950
   b. 1966
   c. 1989
   d. 1996

2. The Baltimore football franchise has, at some point, been in both the American Football Conference and the National Football Conference.

   a. True
   b. False

3. Which two factors played the most significant role in the choice of the nickname "Ravens" for Baltimore's football team?

   a. A recall of the city's wheelchair basketball team name and the idea of building a rivalry with other bird-based NFL teams like the Eagles, Falcons, and Seahawks

b. The fierce image of the bird circling over fallen enemies and the desire for an image that symbolized an aerial attack as opposed to a ground-based offense

c. An homage to a famous poem written in the city and the association with another bird used for the city's baseball team, the Orioles

d. The name of the owner's daughter and a financial connection with a Baltimore-based software company, Raven Technology

4. In which season did the Ravens move from their temporary home and begin to play in their new stadium (M&T Bank Stadium)?

   a. 1996
   b. 1998
   c. 2007
   d. 2015

5. Who is considered the founder of the Baltimore Ravens?

   a. Art Modell
   b. Stephen Bisciotti
   c. Paul Brown
   d. Ozzie Newsome

6. In which season did the Ravens finish second in the AFC Central to earn their first-ever playoff berth?

   a. 1996
   b. 1998

    c. 2000

    d. 2002

7. Counting both regular season and playoffs, the Baltimore Ravens won more games than any other NFL team from 2000 through 2010.

    a. True

    b. False

8. How many division titles have the Ravens won?

    a. 3

    b. 4

    c. 5

    d. 6

9. Who was the first Raven ever to be named a first-team All-Pro?

    a. Linebacker Ray Lewis

    b. Offensive tackle Jonathan Ogden

    c. Safety Ed Reed

    d. Wide receiver Jermaine Lewis

10. Where do the Baltimore Ravens rank in Super Bowl championships won?

    a. First in the NFL

    b. Fourth in the NFL

    c. Tied for 10th in the NFL

    d. Tied for 18th in the NFL

11. How did the Ravens fare during their celebrated 10th anniversary season in the NFL?

a. Missed the playoffs with a 6-10 record

b. Lost in the first round of the playoffs to the New England Patriots

c. Lost in the Super Bowl to the San Francisco 49ers

d. Won the Super Bowl over the New York Giants

12. According to a *Forbes Magazine* evaluation, the Baltimore Ravens are the highest valued sports franchise in the American Football Conference at $2.7 billion and rank behind only the Dallas Cowboys league-wide.

a. True

b. False

13. Which team did the Ravens face in their first-ever NFL game (which resulted in a 19-14 victory for Baltimore)?

a. Tennessee Titans

b. San Diego Chargers

c. Oakland Raiders

d. Cincinnati Bengals

14. What were the details surrounding the time the Ravens' defense pitched its first-ever shutout in the NFL?

a. 1996, in their first season, a 12-0 victory over the Kansas City Chiefs

b. 2004, in their ninth season, a 38-0 victory over the Washington Redskins

c. 2011, in their sixteenth season, a 52-0 victory over the Denver Broncos

d. 1999, in their fourth season, a 22-0 victory over the Cincinnati Bengals

15. Which player kicked the first-ever successful field goal for the Baltimore Ravens?

    a. Matt Stover
    b. Billy Cundiff
    c. Shayne Graham
    d. Stephen Hauschka

16. The Ravens have sent more players to the Pro Bowl to represent Baltimore than any other NFL franchise.

    a. True
    b. False

17. How did Baltimore fare in its first-ever NFL playoff run?

    a. Lost in the wildcard playoffs to the Denver Broncos
    b. Lost in the divisional playoffs to the Pittsburgh Steelers
    c. Lost in the conference championship to the New England Patriots
    d. Won the Super Bowl over the New York Giants

18. The shortest ownership term for a Baltimore Ravens owner is held by Art Modell. For how long did he own the team?

    a. 3 years
    b. 6 years
    c. 9 years
    d. 12 years

19. Which famous author, whose gravesite is in Baltimore, wrote the poem that gave the team its name?

a. Mark Twain

b. Ernest Hemingway

c. Edgar Allan Poe

d. F. Scott Fitzgerald

20. In the Ravens' inaugural season, they played 10 games that were decided by a single possession and posted a 3-7 record in those games.

a. True

b. False

QUIZ ANSWERS

1. D – 1996

2. B – False

3. C – An homage to a famous poem written in the city and the association with another bird used for the city's baseball team, the Orioles

4. B – 1998

5. A – Art Modell

6. C – 2000

7. B – False

8. D – 6

9. B – Offensive tackle Jonathan Ogden

10. C – Tied for 10th in the NFL

11. A – Missed the playoffs with a 6-10 record

12. B – False

13. C – Oakland Raiders

14. D – 1999, in their fourth season, a 22-0 victory over the Cincinnati Bengals

15. A – Matt Stover

16. B – False

17. D – Won the Super Bowl over the New York Giants

18. C – 9 years

19. C – Edgar Allan Poe

20. A – True

DID YOU KNOW?

1. M&T Bank Stadium, the current home of the Ravens, is directly adjacent to the home of Major League Baseball's Baltimore Orioles, Oriole Park at Camden Yards. The stadium was originally called Ravens Stadium at Camden Yards before naming rights were sold in 1999. M&T Bank owns these rights through 2027.

2. Before the Ravens, Baltimore had been home to another NFL franchise, the Baltimore Colts. The Colts played in the NFL for 30 years. They won three NFL championships in the pre-Super Bowl era and they also won Super Bowl V before moving to Indianapolis. Their franchise records moved with the team to Indianapolis and are not considered part of the Ravens' history.

3. The first touchdown in Raven history was scored on a 9-yard rush by quarterback Vinny Testaverde. The score gave Baltimore a 7 – 0 lead in an eventual 19-14 win over the Oakland Raiders in 1996. Earnest Byner scored the winning touchdown on a 1-yard rush in the fourth quarter, sending the fans into a frenzy.

4. M&T Bank Stadium is one of the most widely praised stadiums in the NFL. While it hosts other events, the Ravens are the primary tenant and every effort is made to provide them with state-of-the-art accommodations. For example, the playing surface updates to a new type of grass on average once every seven years.

5. Since the Ravens moved to Baltimore from Cleveland, they were not required to pay the usual expansion fee associated with a new team. Instead, owner Art Modell was required to pay a $29 million relocation fee to the NFL. As part of the agreement, all team records and history remained the property of Cleveland and were restored to the Cleveland Browns when they were granted a replacement team years later.

6. In addition to their mascot, Poe, Baltimore has two real ravens named Rise and Conquer, who appear before kickoff and on the sidelines during many Ravens games. The birds are brothers who live at the Maryland Zoo when they are not at football games or other events.

7. Baltimore's biggest NFL rival is generally thought to be the Pittsburgh Steelers because the two teams have consistently fought for supremacy in the AFC North Division. The Steelers have the advantage in the head-to-head rivalry, 29 – 24, but both teams have won two Super Bowls since the beginning of the rivalry.

8. Baltimore's franchise record for most victories in a single regular season is 14, which they set during the 2019 season behind an MVP campaign from quarterback Lamar Jackson.

9. The Ravens have had only three head coaches in their franchise history: Ted Marchibroda, Brian Billick, and the current head coach, John Harbaugh.

10.

11. In the beginning, the Ravens struggled under Ted Marchibroda. In both of their first two seasons, the team finished last in their division. In their third season, they finished second last, so Marchibroda was let go and replaced with Brian Billick, who lasted nine seasons.

CHAPTER 2:

JERSEYS & NUMBERS

QUIZ TIME!

1. When they began playing in the NFL, the Ravens used what color scheme for their uniforms?

    a. Red, white, and navy blue
    b. Brown, orange, and white
    c. Purple, black, and metallic gold
    d. Black, gray, and white

2. The numbers 0 and 00 have been banned from circulation by Baltimore's ownership because they are seen to represent a losing attitude.

    a. True
    b. False

3. In which year did the Ravens prohibit white cleats and switch to wearing only black cleats to better fit the "Raven" color motif?

    a. 1999
    b. 2002

c. 2007

d. 2018

4. Two excellent Baltimore linebackers wore numbers 52 and 55 for over a decade with the team. Who were these two linebackers?

    a. Ray Lewis and Terrell Suggs

    b. Adalius Thomas and Ray Lewis

    c. Terrell Suggs and Peter Boulware

    d. Bart Scott and Peter Boulware

5. Why did star Ravens kicker Justin Tucker choose No. 9?

    a. He was a fan of Detroit Red Wings hockey star Gordie Howe, who wore the number.

    b. He was a fan of Brazilian soccer star Ronaldo, who wore the number.

    c. He was a fan of Boston Red Sox baseball star Ted Williams, who wore the number.

    d. He was a fan of San Antonio Spurs basketball star Tony Parker, who wore the number.

6. Which jersey has proven to be most popular with Ravens fans in 2020, having been purchased more times than all but three others, league-wide on NFL.com?

    a. Justin Tucker's No. 9

    b. Patrick Queen's No. 48

    c. J.K. Dobbin's No. 27

    d. Lamar Jackson's No. 8

7. Young Ravens cornerback Marlon Humphrey wears No. 44 on his jersey in honor of his father, Bobby Humphrey,

who wore the number as an NFL running back with the Miami Dolphins.

a. True

b. False

8. Five players have worn No. 99 for the Ravens. Which defensive end had the highest-numbered jersey in Baltimore franchise history for the longest time?

a. Paul Kruger

b. Matt Judon

c. Chris Canty

d. Michael McCrary

9. The current version of the Ravens uniform includes three colors. Which of the following is NOT included in the color scheme?

a. Purple

b. Black

c. Silver

d. Gold

10. Punter Sam Koch is the only Raven to ever wear which uniform number for more than a single season in Baltimore?

a. 4

b. 6

c. 77

d. 00

11. Twelve players have worn No. 33 for the Ravens. Which of these players scored the most career touchdowns while sporting that number?

    a. Running back Le'Ron McLain

    b. Running back Bam Morris

    c. Safety Will Hill

    d. Running back Priest Holmes

12. Star quarterback Joe Flacco is not just the only QB, but also the only Raven to have ever worn the No. 5 on his jersey for Baltimore.

    a. True

    b. False

13. Why did highly drafted quarterback Robert Griffin III choose to wear No. 3 on the back of his jersey when he came to Baltimore?

    a. Baltimore was the third team he was playing with in the NFL.

    b. He was three years removed from a traumatic leg injury that had interrupted his promising career.

    c. It represented the Holy Trinity (the Father, the Son, and the Holy Spirit).

    d. The number represented his three children (Robert IV, Latisha, and DeShaun).

14. How many jersey numbers have the Baltimore Ravens retired to honor former players?

    a. 0

    b. 3

c. 4

d. 5

15. Which player competed for the Ravens for four seasons, the longest tenure of anyone who has worn the No. 2 for the franchise?

    a. Quarterback Jimmy Clausen

    b. Quarterback Tyrod Taylor

    c. Quarterback Anthony Wright

    d. Kicker Stephen Hauschka

16. Only one player has ever worn No. 1 for Baltimore. That was quarterback Randall Cunningham, who was allowed to use it only during his final NFL season.

    a. True

    b. False

17. Lucky No. 7 has been worn by five Ravens players over the years. Which player wore it for the longest time?

    a. Quarterback Trace McSorley

    b. Kicker Billy Cundiff

    c. Quarterback Chris Redman

    d. Quarterback Kyle Boller

18. Who is the most recent Ravens player to have his number retired by the club, and in which year was this number retired?

    a. Linebacker Ray Lewis in 2013

    b. Quarterback Steve McNair in 2016

    c. Safety Ed Reed in 2018

    d. The Ravens have never retired a jersey number.

19. Which number did Baltimore quarterback Vinny Testaverde, who was named the first starting QB in Ravens history, wear?

    a. 7
    b. 9
    c. 12
    d. 19

20. The Ravens have retired more jersey numbers than any other NFL franchise has, despite being in existence for many fewer decades than most teams.

    a. True
    b. False

QUIZ ANSWERS

1. C – Purple, black, and metallic gold

2. B – False

3. C – 2007

4. A – Ray Lewis and Terrell Suggs

5. B – He was a fan of Brazilian soccer star Ronaldo, who wore the number.

6. D – Lamar Jackson's No. 8

7. A – True

8. D – Michael McCrary

9. C – Silver

10. A – No. 4

11. D – Running back Priest Holmes

12. B – False

13. C – It represented the Holy Trinity (the Father, the Son, and the Holy Spirit).

14. A – 0

15. B – Quarterback Tyrod Taylor

16. A – True

17. D – Kyle Boller

18. D – The Ravens have never retired a jersey number.

19. C – No. 12

20. B – False

DID YOU KNOW?

1. When they first joined the NFL, the Ravens used a "Flying B" logo for their first three seasons. It was a shield with "Ravens" written across the top and a large "B" underneath, along with wings spreading out from each side. Baltimore switched to a Raven's-head logo in 1999, which is what is currently seen on their uniforms and merchandise.

2. In 2004, the Ravens introduced an all-black alternate uniform. In addition to black pants, helmets, socks, cleats, and jerseys, the uniforms featured white numbers and names with gold trim around the lettering.

3. Four times in their existence, the Ravens have worn a commemorative patch on their jerseys. They displayed one for each of the two Super Bowls they had won, as well as a different patch for their 10th- and 20th-anniversary seasons.

4. Ravens offensive lineman Ben Powers enjoys his No. 72 jersey because, he claims, "sharp numbers like a 7 and a 2 look a lot better on an offensive lineman than a round number like a 0."

5. In 2015, Baltimore wore gold pants and purple jerseys for a game. The look was not well received by players or fans, and that remains the only time the team has worn gold pants.

6. Hall of Fame safety Ed Reed wore No. 20 for the Ravens, the same number he had worn while starring in college as a Miami Hurricane. Reed felt that he had achieved great success (including winning the NCAA championship) with the number in college, so there was no need to change it and risk bad luck after turning pro.

7. Superstition may have scared some Ravens away from wearing the No. 13. Only four players in franchise history have chosen it for themselves, with no Baltimore player sporting the number until 2015. It does not seem to have been lucky, as none of these four players wore it for more than a single season.

8. Since 1973, the NFL no longer allows players to wear jersey No. 0 or 00. The Baltimore Ravens did not enter the league until 1996, which means that no Ravens player will ever wear either number.

9. The Ravens set a new franchise high in 2018, when the team wore 10 distinctly different uniforms during the season, including new pants that were predominantly purple, but with both black and white stripes down the legs.

10. In the 2018 NFL draft, the Ravens selected two tight ends, Hayden Hurst of South Carolina and Mark Andrews of Oklahoma. Both wanted to wear No. 81 with Baltimore but Hurst was given the right to the number since he was taken earlier in the draft. Andrews had to settle for No. 89 instead.

CHAPTER 3:

CATCHY NICKNAMES

QUIZ TIME!

1. A very popular song by which rock star is referenced every time the Baltimore Ravens are referred to by their team nickname, "Purple Pain"?

    a. Michael Jackson
    b. Steven Tyler
    c. Prince
    d. George Michael

2. When he was a child, Ravens wide receiver John Brown was given the nickname "Smokey" by his grandmother because of the color of his skin.

    a. True
    b. False

3. The long-time home of the Ravens, M&T Bank Stadium, is also more commonly known to fans and ticketholders by which popular nickname?

    a. "The ATM"
    b. "The Ravens' Nest"

c. "The Cornfield"

d. "The Big Crab Cake"

4. Which Baltimore player, who is chock full of personality, is affectionately known by players and fans by the moniker "T-Sizzle"?

    a. Quarterback Trace McSorley

    b. Tight end Todd Heap

    c. Linebacker Terrell Suggs

    d. Defensive tackle Tony Siragusa

5. Why was Ravens linebacker Ray Lewis known around the league as "Brickwall"?

    a. He covered so much of the field that ball carriers felt like there was a wall running from sideline to sideline.

    b. He tackled opposing players so hard that it felt like running into a brick wall.

    c. He could not be intimidated, and any attempts at trash talking we shut down immediately as if the insults hit a brick wall.

    d. He once got into a fight with a teammate in practice and smashed his teammate's head into a brick wall.

6. Which of the following is NOT a nickname that was given to one of the members of the Ravens 2019 rookie class?

    a. "Biggie"

    b. "Sack Daddy"

    c. "Mack Truck"

    d. "Smack Down"

7. After Ravens running back Ray Rice was suspended by the NFL for a domestic violence incident, he was labeled "Sugar" Ray Rice in reference to the famous boxers "Sugar" Ray Leonard and "Sugar" Ray Robinson.

   a. True
   b. False

8. Why was future Ravens running back Javorius Allen given the nickname "Buck" by his high school teammates?

   a. Even in high school, he talked incessantly about the NFL contracts he'd be signing one day, making him "all about the bucks."
   b. The term "Buck" was an acceptable version of a swear word that Allen was very fond of using in practice.
   c. He would challenge defensive players to tackle him one on one, often asking "wanna put a buck on it?"
   d. He played as a freshman on the varsity team, so his teammates thought of him as a "young buck."

9. The Ravens share a nickname with which popular flavor of Gatorade, the drink that replenishes electrolytes and is found on sidelines throughout the NFL?

   a. "Arctic Blitz"
   b. "Icy Charge"
   c. "Blackberry Wave"
   d. "Riptide Rush"

10. Beloved Ravens defensive tackle Tony Siragusa went by which one-word nickname when he was referenced by people who knew him well?

a. "Tone"

b. "Wall"

c. "Goose"

d. "Stud"

11. Which Ravens defensive back was known to fans and teammates by the complimentary nickname "Ball Hawk," which referenced his ability to bait the opposing quarterback into throwing ill-advised passed that he could then intercept?

    a. Cornerback Jimmy Smith

    b. Safety Eric Weddle

    c. Cornerback Rod Woodson

    d. Safety Ed Reed

12. Ravens wide receiver Anquan Boldin was known to teammates by a single letter, but rather than using "A" or "B", Boldin went by "Q".

    a. True

    b. False

13. Which current Raven receiver is known to teammates by the nickname "Hollywood"?

    a. Willie Snead IV

    b. Miles Boykin

    c. Devin Duvernay

    d. Marquise Brown

14. Humongous Ravens offensive lineman Orlando Brown was nicknamed after which mythical strong man?

a. "Zeus"

b. "Apollo"

c. "Titan"

d. "Hercules"

15. What is the collective nickname for the group of football fans who attend home games or otherwise cheer for Baltimore?

a. "The Crabheads"

b. "The Ravens Flock"

c. "The Baltimore Boys"

d. "The Raven Lunatics"

16. Ravens defensive lineman Terrence Cody was such a large presence that he often took on two blockers at once and earned himself the nickname "Mount Cody."

a. True

b. False

17. What is the content of the NFL rule that is commonly known as "The Tucker Rule," named after Baltimore kicker Justin Tucker?

a. A kicker may not approach the ball from more than five steps back when attempting a field goal.

b. If a kicker attempts to advance the ball on a fake field goal attempt, there will be no roughing the kicker penalty assessed should he be tackled by the defense.

c. If a football is kicked directly over one of the goalposts, it will count as a successful field goal attempt.

d. When a team attempts to go for an extra point kick after a touchdown is scored, they must attempt it from a 33-yard distance (since 2015).

18. Linebacker Terrell Suggs famously claimed in a celebrated interview that he went to which school before being drafted by the Ravens in 2003?

    a. "The School of Hard Knocks"
    b. "Ball So Hard University"
    c. "Cocaine College"
    d. "Linebacker U"

19. Ravens kicker Stephen Hauschka was dubbed what after converting many field goals in key situations?

    a. "Hausch Money"
    b. "Bet the Hausch"
    c. "Steve-o-Matic"
    d. "Stevie Three"

20. Baltimore defensive lineman Kelly Gregg received the nickname "Buddy Lee" because his appearance matched a Levi Jeans mascot by that name and teammates found this fact hilarious.

    a. True
    b. False

QUIZ ANSWERS

1. C – Prince

2. A – True

3. D – "The Big Crab Cake"

4. C – Linebacker Terrell Suggs

5. B – He tackled opposing players so hard that it felt like running into a brick wall.

6. D – "Smack Down"

7. B – False

8. D – He played as a freshman on the varsity team, so his teammates thought of him as a "young buck."

9. D – "Riptide Rush"

10. C – "Goose"

11. D – Safety Ed Reed

12. A – True

13. D – Marquise Brown

14. A – Zeus

15. B – "The Ravens Flock"

16. A – True

17. C – If a football is kicked directly over one of the goalposts, it will count as a successful field goal attempt.

18. B – "Ball So Hard University"

19. A – "Hausch Money"

20. A – True

DID YOU KNOW?

1. When Baltimore was considering a nickname for its football team, the *Baltimore Sun* ran a fan poll in which over 33,000 voters responded. "Ravens" was easily the top choice with over 63% of the vote, beating out "Americans" and "Marauders," which were the next top choices.

2. Current Baltimore defensive coordinator Don Martindale is known around the NFL as "Wink," in reference to the popular game show host Wink Martindale, who served as the host on such game shows as *Tic-Tac-Dough*, *High Rollers*, *Gambit*, and *Debt*.

3. Although a group of ravens is called an "unkindness," Baltimore's team is often referred to as "Purple Murder." A "murder" is the name for a group of crows, but the term was definitely catchier and it tied into one of author and team inspiration Edgar Allan Poe's favorite themes. Therefore, "Purple Murder" stuck.

4. During the team's first two NFL seasons, they played home games at Memorial Stadium, which had two nicknames: "The Old Gray Lady of 33rd Street" in general, and "The World's Largest Outdoor Insane Asylum" specifically for football games.

5. Ravens quarterback Steve McNair shared a nickname with basketball legend Michael Jordan. Both were known as "Air," though McNair earned the moniker for his throwing

arm rather than his hang time and didn't reach the level of fame Jordan did, despite winning an NFL MVP Award.

6. Baltimore's Tyrod Taylor did not have the biggest throwing arm, but he was able to scramble and buy some time by avoiding pass rushers. This led to the quarterback being nicknamed after an American wireless phone company: "T-Mobile."

7. One common nickname for the Baltimore Ravens refers to their power and fierceness without leaving much hope for opponents: "Death on Wings."

8. When Ravens coach John Harbaugh led the team to the Super Bowl in 2013, he faced a familiar foe on the San Francisco 49ers sideline: his brother Jim. Media figures commonly referred to this battle between brothers as "The Harbaugh Bowl" or "HarBowl."

9. Ravens QB Joe Flacco shares a nickname with another all-time great NFL player. Both he and 49ers quarterback Joe Montana were known as "Joe Cool" for their ability to remain calm and perform under pressure. While Montana was much emulated though, Flacco's staid demeanor was not seen by many as "cool."

10. Former Ravens tight end Shannon Sharpe was a star on the field but did not receive his nickname "Unc" until he became a star on the set of his television show *Skip and Shannon: Undisputed.*

CHAPTER 4:

RAVENS QUARTERBACKS

QUIZ TIME!

1. Which mobile Baltimore QB holds the NFL record for most rushing yards gained in a season by a quarterback?

   a. Randall Cunningham

   b. Steve McNair

   c. Vinny Testaverde

   d. Lamar Jackson

2. Joe Flacco holds the top four spots on the Ravens' all-time list of passing touchdowns thrown in a season.

   a. True

   b. False

3. Which quarterback has thrown the most interceptions in Baltimore Ravens franchise history?

   a. Vinny Testaverde

   b. Elvis Grbac

   c. Joe Flacco

   d. Kyle Boller

4. Which of these Ravens quarterbacks has been sacked by opponents the most times (333)?

   a. Jeff Blake
   b. Trent Dilfer
   c. Kyle Boller
   d. Joe Flacco

5. Baltimore quarterback Jimmy Clausen appeared as the subject of an article in *Sports Illustrated* magazine while he was still a junior in high school. What was the title of the article?

   a. "Coveted Clausen Considers College Commitment"
   b. "The Kid with the Golden Arm"
   c. "17 and Undefeated"
   d. "Jimmy Clausen Follows in Brothers' Footsteps"

6. Against which team did quarterback Kyle Boller lead the Ravens to a 48-3 victory on December 19th, 2005, in the process setting the *Monday Night Football* record for most lopsided victory?

   a. Green Bay Packers
   b. Cleveland Browns
   c. New England Patriots
   d. New York Giants

7. Lamar Jackson has played more games at QB for the Ravens than any other player in franchise history.

   a. True
   b. False

8. Who is the Baltimore Ravens all-time career leader in passing yards?

    a. Joe Flacco
    b. Vinny Testaverde
    c. Lamar Jackson
    d. Steve McNair

9. Who set the franchise record for most passing yards in a single season?

    a. Steve McNair
    b. Joe Flacco
    c. Lamar Jackson
    d. Jeff Blake

10. Which of the following is NOT a fact about Ravens quarterback Vinny Testaverde?

    a. He has more passing yards and more touchdown passes than any quarterbacks who are eligible but have not been inducted into the Pro Football Hall of Fame.
    b. He has the Ravens record for most game-winning drives in a single season.
    c. He has more losses as a starting QB than any other player in NFL history.
    d. He has completed an NFL pass to more players than any other quarterback.

11. How many times did prolific Ravens quarterback Joe Flacco throw for 20 or more touchdowns in a season?

a. 2

b. 4

c. 6

d. 8

12. Among quarterbacks who have played at least ten games in a season with Baltimore, Trent Dilfer has the highest interception percentage, 4.9% in 2000.

    a. True

    b. False

13. Which Ravens quarterback became an ordained Protestant minister after retiring from his NFL playing career and started his own church in Las Vegas before becoming an NFL team chaplain?

    a. Trent Dilfer

    b. Stoney Case

    c. Elvis Grbac

    d. Randall Cunningham

14. How many former Raven quarterbacks have been elected to the Pro Football Hall of Fame?

    a. 0

    b. 1

    c. 2

    d. 4

15. When Baltimore quarterback Lamar Jackson's speed was rated a 96 in 2019 for the Madden NFL video game series, he became the fastest QB in the history of the game, surpassing which former leader in the category?

a. Cam Newton of the Carolina Panthers

b. Randall Cunningham of the Philadelphia Eagles

c. Steve Young of the San Francisco 49ers

d. Michael Vick of the Atlanta Falcons

16. Ravens QB Trent Dilfer won a high school state championship, a college football national championship, and a Super Bowl championship.

a. True

b. False

17. Two Ravens quarterbacks have played for seven NFL teams, more than any other franchise leader. Who were these well-traveled players?

a. Trent Dilfer and Tyrod Taylor

b. Matt Schaub and Scott Mitchell

c. Jeff Blake and Vinny Testaverde

d. Tony Banks and Joe Flacco

18. Which Raven was the youngest player in team history to start at quarterback, at the age of 21?

a. Robert Griffin III

b. Lamar Jackson

c. Eric Zeier

d. Chris Redman

19. "January Joe" Flacco always performed better in the playoffs for the Ravens, and in fact holds the NFL postseason record for which of the following stats?

a. Most postseason touchdown passes thrown by a quarterback in a winning effort

b. Highest completion percentage increase between regular season and postseason

c. Most postseason road victories by a quarterback

d. Fewest postseason interceptions thrown by a quarterback with a minimum of 10 starts

20. Ravens QB Lamar Jackson named Joe Flacco as the godfather when his daughter Shauna was born in 2018.

a. True

b. False

QUIZ ANSWERS

1. D – Lamar Jackson

2. B – False

3. C – Joe Flacco

4. D – Joe Flacco

5. B – "The Kid with the Golden Arm"

6. A – Green Bay Packers

7. B – False

8. A – Joe Flacco

9. B – Joe Flacco

10. B – He has the Ravens record for most game-winning drives in a single season.

11. C – 6

12. A – True

13. D – Randall Cunningham

14. A – 0

15. D – Michael Vick of the Atlanta Falcons

16. B – False

17. C – Jeff Blake and Vinny Testaverde

18. B – Lamar Jackson

19. C – Most postseason road victories by a quarterback

20. B – False

DID YOU KNOW?

1. When Jim Harbaugh played quarterback for the Baltimore Ravens in 1998, little did he know that he would not be the most famous family member in the organization's history. His brother John Harbaugh became the team's coach in 2008 and is still there today.

2. No Ravens quarterback has ever been able to complete 70% of his passes in a season. The most accurate was Lamar Jackson, who came the closest in 2019, when he reached 66.1%.

3. Joe Flacco owns the longest passing play in Ravens history. In 2016, he dropped back and found talented receiver Mike Wallace for a 95-yard touchdown toss that led Baltimore to a 21-14 victory over Wallace's former team, the Pittsburgh Steelers.

4. In one forgettable game against the Kansas City Chiefs in 1999, Ravens quarterback Stoney Case threw for 103 passing yards on the day. Unfortunately, the Chiefs ran back interceptions thrown by Case for 108 yards and two touchdowns, leaving Case with net negative yardage on the day.

5. Tony Banks could have used some better blocking when he became the Ravens QB in 1999. He was sacked a whopping 9.3% of the time he dropped back to pass, the

highest rate in Baltimore history for a quarterback who started the majority of the team's games.

6. Only one quarterback has played his entire NFL career with Baltimore. Wally Richardson spent just one season with the franchise, in 1998, and threw only 2 passes. Current quarterback Lamar Jackson has not played anywhere else in his three-year NFL career, but it remains to be seen if he will retire as a Raven.

7. Quarterback Trent Dilfer spent six years with the Tampa Bay Buccaneers, four years with the Seattle Seahawks, and one year each with the Cleveland Browns and the San Francisco 49ers, during which time he competed in just two playoff games. Dilfer played only one season with the Ravens and he led the team to its first-ever Super Bowl victory.

8. Future Ravens quarterback Elvis Grbac was declared *People* magazine's Sexiest Athlete in 1998. However, he won the title accidentally: The photographer meant to take a picture of starter Rich Gannon but ended up with Grbac by mistake.

9. During the 2013 season, quarterback Joe Flacco started the Ravens' home opener against the Cleveland Browns and threw a touchdown pass to lead them to victory. There would be nothing remarkable about this...except that Flacco's wife Dana had given birth to the couple's son Daniel about one hour before game time!

10. Flacco had the longest tenure as Ravens QB. He spent a full decade with the team from 2008 to 2018 and played in 163 games. That's more than any Raven regardless of position, except for punter Sam Koch.

CHAPTER 5:

THE PASS CATCHERS

QUIZ TIME!

1. Which Ravens pass catcher holds the franchise record for most receiving yards in a single postseason game?

    a. Tight end Todd Heap

    b. Wide receiver Torrey Smith

    c. Tight end Shannon Sharpe

    d. Wide receiver Anquan Boldin

2. No one is within 100 receptions of wide receiver Derrick Mason at the top of Baltimore's record book.

    a. True

    b. False

3. Six wide receivers have recorded over 15 career touchdown catches for the Ravens. Which one of them has the most?

    a. Michael Jackson

    b. Qadry Ismail

    c. Derrick Mason

    d. Torrey Smith

4. Who is the Ravens single-season leader in receiving touchdowns scored, with 14?

   a. Michael Jackson
   b. Torrey Smith
   c. Derrick Alexander
   d. Derrick Mason

5. Who holds the all-time career franchise record for receiving yardage for the Ravens?

   a. Wide receiver Mark Clayton
   b. Wide receiver Qadry Ismail
   c. Wide receiver Derrick Mason
   d. Tight end Todd Heap

6. How did Baltimore tight end Dennis Pitta suffer the injury that put an end to his NFL career?

   a. Suffered a concussion while being tackled out of bounds on a late hit
   b. Shot in the leg during an armed robbery at the team's hotel
   c. Injured his hip for the third time during a non-contact play
   d. Broke a vertebra while diving into shallow water on vacation

7. Tight end Shannon Sharpe had more catches in each of his two years with the Ravens than he did in any of his 12 years with the Denver Broncos.

   a. True
   b. False

8. Which two Ravens wide receivers with at least 100 receptions averaged 15 yards per catch over their careers?

    a. Torrey Smith and Derrick Alexander
    b. Qadry Ismail and Steve Smith
    c. Anquan Boldin and Derrick Mason
    d. Jermaine Lewis and Michael Jackson

9. Which pass catcher has played more games with the franchise than any other pass catcher?

    a. Tight end Nick Boyle
    b. Wide receiver Jermaine Lewis
    c. Tight end Todd Heap
    d. Wide receiver Derrick Mason

10. Three pass catchers have racked up over 300 career receptions for the Baltimore Ravens. Which of the following players is NOT in that club?

    a. Wide receiver Torrey Smith
    b. Running back Ray Rice
    c. Tight end Todd Heap
    d. Wide receiver Derrick Mason

11. From which rival team did the Ravens poach star wide receiver Derrick Mason when they signed him as a free agent in 2005?

    a. Houston Texans
    b. Arizona Cardinals
    c. San Diego Chargers
    d. Tennessee Titans

12. Baltimore wide receiver Jermaine Lewis holds the Ravens franchise records for most kickoff returns, most punt returns, most punt return yards, and most punt return touchdowns.

    a. True
    b. False

13. Despite all his accomplishments, Jermaine Lewis has more career fumbles than any other Ravens wide receiver. How many times did he cough up the ball?

    a. 8
    b. 10
    c. 11
    d. 13

14. Marquise Brown signed the highest contract given out by Baltimore to a current wide receiver. How much is his contract worth?

    a. $7,500,612 over 2 years
    b. $9,250,000 over 3 years
    c. $11,787,340 over 4 years
    d. $13,999,999 over 5 years

15. How many Ravens tight ends have caught over 200 passes for the club during their careers?

    a. One: Todd Heap
    b. Two: Todd Heap and Dennis Pitta
    c. Three: Todd Heap, Dennis Pitta, and Shannon Sharpe
    d. Four: Todd Heap, Dennis Pitta, Shannon Sharpe, and Mark Andrews

16. Ravens wide receiver Mark Clayton is not the first NFL wide receiver to go by that name. Another Mark Clayton, born 21 years earlier, starred for the Miami Dolphins but retired before Baltimore's Clayton began his career.

   a. True
   b. False

17. Which wide receiver loved his time in Baltimore so much that he signed a one-day contract to retire with the franchise after playing for two other teams after having left the Ravens?

   a. Anquan Boldin
   b. Steve Smith
   c. Derrick Mason
   d. Derrick Alexander

18. Wide receiver Qadry Ismail holds the franchise record for most receiving yards in a single game, set in 1999 against the Pittsburgh Steelers. How many yards did he accumulate?

   a. 174 yards
   b. 196 yards
   c. 211 yards
   d. 258 yards

19. Which two teammates posted the highest combined receiving yardage total in a season for the Ravens?

   a. Torrey Smith and Anquan Boldin in 2012
   b. Willie Snead and Michael Crabtree in 2018

c. Michael Jackson and Derrick Alexander in 1996

d. Derrick Mason and Anquan Boldin in 2010

20. Ravens tight end Mark Andrews has Type 1 diabetes and wears an insulin pump under specially designed padding while playing football. He is the only NFL player to date to do so.

   a. True

   b. False

QUIZ ANSWERS

1. D – Wide receiver Anquan Boldin

2. B – False

3. D – Torrey Smith

4. A – Michael Jackson

5. C – Wide receiver Derrick Mason

6. C – Injured his hip for the third time during a non-contact play

7. B – False

8. A – Torrey Smith and Derrick Alexander

9. C – Tight end Todd Heap

10. A – Wide receiver Torrey Smith

11. D – Tennessee Titans

12. A – True

13. D – 13

14. C – $11,787,340 over 4 years

15. B – Two: Todd Heap and Dennis Pitta

16. A – True

17. C – Derrick Mason

18. D – 258 yards

19. C – Michael Jackson and Derrick Alexander in 1996

20. B – False

DID YOU KNOW?

1. Wide receiver Derrick Alexander is the Ravens franchise leader in career receiving yards per game. Alexander averaged 70.3 yards per game and remains the only Baltimore player to put up over 70 in that category.

2. Ravens pass catcher Steve Smith ranks 8th on the all-time list for most receiving yards in NFL history. Anquan Boldin is 14th on the list, though both were a little past their prime when playing for Baltimore.

3. Although Dennis Pitta went on to have a very good career with the Ravens, his debut in 2010 carried about as little impact as possible. Pitta made one catch all season, for just 1 yard.

4. Tight end Todd Heap became the Baltimore Ravens' broadcast analyst after his retirement, following in the footsteps of the player he backed up during his early years in Baltimore. Shannon Sharpe also went into broadcasting after his retirement.

5. In 2013, Ravens wideout Torrey Smith interned for Elijah Cummings, a member of the United States House of Representatives out of Maryland. Smith addressed both the Maryland State Senate and the Maryland House of Delegates during his time with Cummings.

6. Wide receiver Travis Taylor was a significant deep threat with Baltimore. In each of his five seasons with the

Ravens, Taylor caught at least one pass that went for 40 yards or longer.

7. When the Ravens signed free agent receiver Steve Smith Sr. away from the Carolina Panthers, Smith announced to the press that when he played his former team "put your goggles on 'cause there's going to be blood and guts everywhere." Smith refrained from violence, but did catch 7 passes, racking up 139 receiving yards and 2 touchdowns in a blowout 38-10 victory over the Panthers.

8. After his retirement from pro football, former Ravens wide receiver Michael Jackson ran for mayor of Tangipahoa, Louisiana, which was Jackson's hometown. He won and served four years in office, from 2009 to 2012.

9. Wide receiver Torrey Smith came in with a bang for Baltimore. The Ravens faced the St. Louis Rams in the third week of Smith's rookie season. In the first quarter of that game alone, Smith caught 3 touchdown passes, becoming the first rookie in NFL history to do so.

10. There are no Ravens wide receivers in the Pro Football Hall of Fame or in the team's Ring of Honor. However, there is one tight end in each institution. Shannon Sharpe has been elected to the Hall of Fame and Todd Heap is in the Ring of Honor.

CHAPTER 6:

RUNNING WILD

QUIZ TIME!

1. Who holds the Ravens single-season rushing record with 2066 yards?

    a. Ray Rice

    b. Jamal Lewis

    c. Lamar Jackson

    d. Willis McGahee

2. In running back Mark Ingram's first game with Baltimore, he scored twice and rushed for 107 yards to lead the Ravens to a 59-10 blowout victory over the Miami Dolphins.

    a. True

    b. False

3. Which running back accumulated the most carries for Baltimore without ever scoring a rushing touchdown?

    a. Charles Evans

    b. Vonta Leach

    c. Moe Williams

    d. Leroy Hoard

4. How many running backs have carried the ball over 1000 times for the Ravens?

    a. 0

    b. 1

    c. 2

    d. 5

5. No Ravens running back has averaged over 100 yards per game during his career. Jamal Lewis is the closest; what is his average?

    a. 85.7 yards per game

    b. 89.9 yards per game

    c. 93.4 yards per game

    d. 99.5 yards per game

6. In which season did running back Justin Forsett record an astonishing 5.4 yards per carry for Baltimore?

    a. 2010

    b. 2012

    c. 2013

    d. 2014

7. It is a Ravens tradition for every running back to tap his helmet against the helmets of the starting offensive linemen following the warmup before a game.

    a. True

    b. False

8. Which of the following is NOT true about quirky Ravens running back Willis McGahee?

    a. He studied criminology at the University of Miami.

    b. He once scored two receiving touchdowns and two rushing touchdowns in the same game for the Ravens, against the Kansas City Chiefs.

    c. He was a team member of the Miami Surge, a mixed-gender squad that competed in the National Pro Grid League.

    d. He appeared as the title character on Season 8 of the television show *The Bachelor*.

9. Which Baltimore running back (with at least 300 carries) has the highest career yards gained per attempt, with 5.1 yards per carry?

    a. Ray Rice

    b. Gus Edwards

    c. Jamal Lewis

    d. Mark Ingram

10. Current Ravens running back Mark Ingram recorded his first NFL rushing touchdown while playing for which NFL team?

    a. Baltimore Ravens

    b. New England Patriots

    c. New Orleans Saints

    d. Green Bay Packers

11. How many of the Ravens' top 10 seasons for rushing touchdowns were recorded by the great Jamal Lewis?

a. One season

b. Three seasons

c. Seven seasons

d. Nine seasons

12. Jamal Lewis had 45 career rushing touchdowns with the Ravens, which is more than the next three highest Baltimore running backs combined.

a. True

b. False

13. Which Baltimore running back has the most career fumbles?

a. Jamal Lewis

b. Chester Taylor

c. Ray Rice

d. Willis McGahee

14. Which Raven had the highest single-season rushing yards per game, with an average of 129.1?

a. Ray Rice

b. Mark Ingram

c. Justin Forsett

d. Jamal Lewis

15. Running back Justin Forsett's tenure with the Ravens came to an end after he suffered a broken arm on a hit by which defensive player?

a. Seattle Seahawks linebacker Bobby Wagner

b. Tennessee Titans defensive end Jevon Kearse

c. St. Louis Rams defensive tackle Aaron Donald

d. Pittsburgh Steelers linebacker James Harrison

16. Running back Chester Taylor has served as a backup to many stars, including Jamal Lewis, Adrian Peterson, and Matt Forte.

    a. True

    b. False

17. What did former Ravens running back Jamal Lewis receive as a gift from owner Stephen Bisciotti after Baltimore won Super Bowl XLVII?

    a. A $500,000 payment to thank him for his contributions in developing the team culture

    b. A lifetime position as a team ambassador, promoting the Ravens at trade shows and events

    c. A championship team ring just like those given to the current players

    d. A brand-new Maserati convertible painted in Ravens colors

18. Which musical instrument can Ravens RB Justin Forsett play?

    a. Electric guitar

    b. Banjo

    c. Trombone

    d. Tenor saxophone

19. Which running back was NOT a member of Baltimore's committee during the 2020 NFL season?

a. Gus Edwards

b. Mark Ingram

c. De'Anthony Thomas

d. J.K. Dobbins

20. Ravens running back Bam Morris was known by that name throughout his NFL career, but his real first name is Byron.

a. True

b. False

QUIZ ANSWERS

1. B – Jamal Lewis

2. A – True

3. C – Moe Williams

4. C – 2

5. A – 85.7 yards per game

6. D – 2014

7. B – False

8. D – He appeared as the title character on Season 8 of the television show *The Bachelor*.

9. B – Gus Edwards

10. C – New Orleans Saints

11. B – Three seasons

12. B – False

13. A – Jamal Lewis

14. D – Jamal Lewis

15. C – St. Louis Rams defensive tackle Aaron Donald

16. A – True

17. C – A championship team ring just like those given to the current players

18. D – Tenor saxophone

19. C – De'Anthony Thomas

20. A – True

DID YOU KNOW?

1. In college, future Ravens running back Jamal Lewis actually completed a pass TO his college quarterback, future Pro Football Hall of Famer Peyton Manning.

2. Long-time Ravens running back Ray Rice's full name is unusual: Raymell Mourice Rice. No other Baltimore player has ever been named Raymell.

3. After retirement, Ravens RB Justin Forsett joined a flag football team that competed in the American Flag Football League. He was not the only Ravens RB to do so, as Bernard Pierce also joined the league, along with other NFL stars such as Michael Vick.

4. In 2016, the Ravens drafted running back Kenneth Dixon from Louisiana Tech with the hopes of making him a workhorse back for the team. Unfortunately, Dixon suffered knee injuries in 2017, 2018, and 2019, ending up on the injured reserve list each time, and Baltimore released him in 2019.

5. Baltimore's Ray Rice had an excellent season in 2009, making the Pro Bowl and being selected to the NFL's All-Pro team. However, he topped even that excellent effort two years later when he equaled those accomplishments while also leading the AFC in touchdowns and the entire NFL in yards from scrimmage.

6. In 2011, the Ravens signed fullback Vonta Leach as a free agent. Leach agreed to an $11 million contract over 3 years that established him as the highest-earning fullback in the entire NFL.

7. No running back who has played for the Ravens has been enshrined in the Pro Football Hall of Fame.

8. In 2015, the Ravens announced the signing of running back Terrance West, who was born in Baltimore. West played three seasons for his hometown team before signing a free-agent contract with the New Orleans Saints in 2018.

9. Former Ravens running back Bam Morris played briefly in the Arena Football League after his NFL career finished. He spent the 2009 season with the Katy Copperheads.

10. Baltimore running back Ray Rice's career was ended after an incident in which security footage of him knocking out his wife became public. Rice was suspended by the NFL and no franchise was willing to offer him a contract after the suspension ended, despite his well-established talent.

CHAPTER 7:

IN THE TRENCHES

QUIZ TIME!

1. The Baltimore defensive record for most sacks in a single game is 11. Against which unfortunate quarterback was this record set?

    a. Ben Roethlisberger of the Pittsburgh Steelers
    b. Nathan Peterman of the Buffalo Bills
    c. Brett Favre of the Green Bay Packers
    d. Marcus Mariota of the Tennessee Titans

2. The late 1990s Baltimore defensive line was so strong that they earned their own nickname: The Purple People Eaters.

    a. True
    b. False

3. Who is the Ravens all-time franchise leader in sacks among defensive linemen with 51?

    a. Pernell McPhee
    b. Trevor Pryce

c. Michael McCrary

d. Elvis Dumervil

4. Defensive tackle Tony Siragusa did some acting after his playing career finished. Which of the following did Siragusa NOT appear in?

    a. The popular HBO mob drama *The Sopranos*

    b. An ad campaign for men's adult diapers

    c. A movie directed by Spike Lee called *25th Hour*

    d. The long-running animated comedy series *The Simpsons*

5. Which of the following internal organs did Ravens defensive end Paul Kruger NOT injure severely during separate adolescent incidents?

    a. His spleen

    b. His kidney

    c. His pancreas

    d. His lung

6. Which two linemen have played more games on the Ravens line of scrimmage than anyone else?

    a. Left tackle Jonathan Ogden and right guard Marshal Yanda

    b. Defensive end Jarret Johnson and nose tackle Kelly Gregg

    c. Nose tackle Haloti Ngata and left guard Edwin Mulitalo

    d. Right tackles Orlando Brown Jr. and Michael Oher

7. The 2016 Baltimore Ravens hold the NFL record for the heaviest combined weight of all starting offensive and defensive linemen.

    a. True
    b. False

8. When Ravens defensive end Matt Judon recorded his first career sack, it came against an opposing quarterback who was injured on the play and missed the rest of the year with a torn ACL. Which quarterback did Judon take out?

    a. Geno Smith of the New York Jets
    b. Michael Vick of the Atlanta Falcons
    c. Drew Brees of the San Diego Chargers
    d. Sam Bradford of the Los Angeles Rams

9. Which offensive lineman played both right and left tackle for the Ravens in the four years leading up to Baltimore's second Super Bowl?

    a. Ronnie Stanley
    b. Michael Oher
    c. Jared Gaither
    d. Jonathan Ogden

10. Which defensive end had two sacks in Super Bowl XLVII that limited San Francisco to settle for field goals, which was critical in the Ravens' nail-biting 34-31 victory?

    a. Arthur Jones
    b. DeAngelo Tyson
    c. Pernell McPhee
    d. Paul Kruger

11. Offensive lineman Jonathan Ogden played his entire NFL career with the Baltimore Ravens after they spent their first-ever draft pick on him in 1996. How long did that career last?

  a. 140 games
  b. 163 games
  c. 171 games
  d. 177 games

12. Orlando Brown and his son Orlando Brown Jr. both played the same position (offensive tackle) for the same team (the Baltimore Ravens) in the NFL.

  a. True
  b. False

13. Ravens mainstay Haloti Ngata played over 130 NFL games with the club as a defensive tackle. Where does he rank in games played all-time for Baltimore?

  a. 3rd overall
  b. 8th overall
  c. 12th overall
  d. 19th overall

14. Which current Ravens defensive lineman has the longest tenure in Baltimore?

  a. Pernell McPhee
  b. Brandon Williams
  c. Patrick Ricard
  d. Matt Judon

15. The most sacks in a single season recorded by a Baltimore Raven is 17. Which defensive end set this record?

    a. Elvis Dumervil
    b. Matt Judon
    c. Michael McCrary
    d. Rob Burnett

16. The Ravens used their first-ever pick on offensive lineman Jonathan Ogden in 1996. They did not use a first-round pick on a defensive lineman for 10 more years, when they selected Haloti Ngata 12th overall in 2006.

    a. True
    b. False

17. For the entire 2019 NFL season, Ravens center Bradley Bozeman and his wife lived where?

    a. In the guest house of Ravens head coach John Harbaugh
    b. In a houseboat anchored at a marina near Baltimore's practice facility
    c. In an auxiliary locker room in the lower levels of M&T Bank Stadium
    d. In a 40-foot luxury RV trailer

18. In high school, future Ravens defensive tackle Tony Siragusa also played which other position for the football team?

    a. Quarterback
    b. Placekicker

c. Tight end

d. Fullback

19. Which opposing lineman once said of Ravens Hall of Fame left tackle Jonathan Ogden, "Jonathan would rip your limbs off, and he'd smile...and wave your arm in front of you"?

    a. Bruce Smith of the Buffalo Bills

    b. Reggie White of the Green Bay Packers

    c. Michael Strahan of the New York Giants

    d. Carlos Dunlap of the Cincinnati Bengals

20. Defensive end Elvis Dumervil was named after rock star Elvis Presley, of whom his dad was a big fan.

    a. True

    b. False

QUIZ ANSWERS

1. D – Marcus Mariota of the Tennessee Titans

2. B – False

3. C – Michael McCrary

4. D – The long-running animated comedy series *The Simpsons*

5. C – His pancreas

6. A – Left tackle Jonathan Ogden and right guard Marshal Yanda

7. B – False

8. A – Geno Smith of the New York Jets

9. B – Michael Oher

10. D – Paul Kruger

11. D – 177 games

12. A – True

13. C – 12th overall

14. B – Brandon Williams

15. A – Elvis Dumervil

16. A – True

17. D – In a 40-foot luxury RV trailer

18. B – Placekicker

19. C – Michael Strahan of the New York Giants

20. A – True

DID YOU KNOW?

1. Ravens offensive tackle Jonathan Ogden was an NCAA champion…in shotput. Ogden won this title in 1996 while with the UCLA Bruins, by putting the shot 19.42 meters.

2. Ravens defender Elvis Dumervil once had 6 sacks in a 2005 game for the Louisville Cardinals against the Kentucky Wildcats, an NCAA record that still stands.

3. Guard Marshall Yanda played his entire career with the Baltimore Ravens. This lasted 12 seasons and included eight Pro Bowl selections and a spot on the NFL 2010s All-Decade Team, as well as a place in the Baltimore Ravens Ring of Honor.

4. Defensive end Rob Burnett recorded 73 career sacks and 1 interception.

5. Ravens defensive tackle Haloti Ngata had a long, distinguished career and went out in style. He retired on his birthday, by posting a picture of himself at the top of Mount Kilimanjaro, showing a banner that read "I'm retiring from the NFL on top."

6. At the end of his career, Jonathan Ogden was tied for the title of tallest player in the NFL with another offensive tackle on the Ravens, Jared Gaither. Each of the two massive men stood 6'9" tall.

7. Two days after signing a contract extension with the Ravens for $112.8 million in 2020 (the highest contract for

an offensive lineman), tackle Ronnie Stanley suffered a season-ending ankle injury.

8. Defensive tackle James Jones played three seasons with the Baltimore Ravens, from 1996 through 1998. During his time with the Ravens and his 10-year career as a whole, Jones did not miss a single game.

9. Ben Grubbs was recruited to Auburn University as a defensive end. Auburn slotted him as a defensive tackle on their roster, then moved him to tight end after a year, and finally switched him to the offensive guard position. He was talented enough there that the Ravens made him their first-round draft pick in 2007.

10. In retirement, defensive end Michael McCrary became a commentator discussing Baltimore football for WBAL-AM radio

CHAPTER 8:

THE BACK SEVEN

QUIZ TIME!

1. From which team did the Ravens sign free agent safety Tony Jefferson in 2017?

    a. Dallas Cowboys

    b. Cleveland Browns

    c. Indianapolis Colts

    d. Arizona Cardinals

2. Three of the top four players drafted by the Ravens who lead the team in career interceptions were from the University of Miami.

    a. True

    b. False

3. Which safety is the franchise's all-time leader in interceptions with 61?

    a. Ed Reed

    b. Eric Weddle

   c. Dawan Landry

   d. Eric Turner

4. Which defender is the only Raven to have returned the interceptions for a touchdown, with 7?

   a. Linebacker Ray Lewis

   b. Cornerback Chris McAlister

   c. Safety Ed Reed

   d. Safety Rod Woodson

5. Although sacks are usually not a high priority for defensive backs in most coaching systems, one Ravens DB excelled at this skill, putting up 7.5 sacks in his career. Who?

   a. Safety Ed Reed

   b. Cornerback Corey Ivy

   c. Cornerback Duane Starks

   d. Cornerback Jimmy Smith

6. Which Ravens defender showed the best nose for the ball by leading the team in career forced fumbles?

   a. Linebacker Terrell Suggs

   b. Safety Ed Reed

   c. Linebacker Ray Lewis

   d. Linebacker Adalius Thomas

7. During the poker craze in the 2010s, members of Baltimore's secondary and linebacking corps held a weekly game where, rather than playing for money, the losers had to tweet embarrassing things about themselves or flattering things about the winners.

a. True

b. False

8. Baltimore defensive back Lardarius Webb is a cousin of which Basketball Hall of Fame player?

   a. Center Patrick Ewing

   b. Forward Kevin Garnett

   c. Guard Mitch Richmond

   d. Guard Spud Webb

9. Linebacker C.J. Mosley led the Ravens in tackles in 2014, 2015, 2017, and 2018. Which player had more than Mosley in 2016?

   a. Linebacker Patrick Onwuasor

   b. Cornerback Lardarius Webb

   c. Safety Tony Jefferson

   d. Linebacker Zack Orr

10. What was the name of the restaurant linebacker Ray Lewis owned in Baltimore 2005-2008?

    a. Father Ray's Sandwich Shack

    b. Brickwall Burgers

    c. Ray Lewis Fool Moon Bar-B-Que

    d. Ray's Raven's Nest

11. A quarterback (Joe Flacco) tops the record books for most fumbles recovered for the Ravens but quarterbacks tend to be cleaning up their own mess when this happens. Which defender has created the most turnovers for Baltimore by scooping up opponents' fumbles?

a. Linebacker Terrell Suggs

b. Linebacker Ray Lewis

c. Cornerback Chris McAlister

d. Safety Ed Reed

12. Former Ravens linebacker Peter Boulware went into politics after his retirement from the team and ran (unsuccessfully) as a Republican for a seat in the Florida House.

a. True

b. False

13. There's a statue of which defensive player outside M&T Bank Stadium?

a. Safety Ed Reed

b. Linebacker Terrell Suggs

c. Linebacker Peter Boulware

d. Linebacker Ray Lewis

14. In addition to a Super Bowl victory with Baltimore, with which other NFL team does long-time Ravens linebacker Terrell Suggs have a championship ring?

a. Kansas City Chiefs

b. Denver Broncos

c. Pittsburgh Steelers

d. New England Patriots

15. Which of the following leagues has Ravens defensive back Corey Ivy NOT played in?

a. The National Football League

b. The Arena Football League

c. The Xtreme Football League

d. The United Football League

16. Superstar Ravens safety Ed Reed was the first player in the history of the NFL to return an interception, a fumble, a punt, and a blocked punt for a touchdown.

a. True

b. False

17. What was the title of superstar Ravens' linebacker Ray Lewis' 2015 autobiography?

a. *Before the Canes and Ravens: The Ray Lewis Story*

b. *My Football Life*

c. *The Art of Leadership: From the Locker Room to the Board Room*

d. *I Feel Like Going On: Life, Game, and Glory*

18. On which show did Ravens linebacker Terrell Suggs play a major guest-starring role?

a. *Friday Night Lights*

b. *Ballers*

c. *Chicago Fire*

d. *The Wire*

19. Which other NFL Hall of Famer did Baltimore's Ray Lewis defeat in an episode of the television show *Lip Sync Battle* after choosing songs by Nelly and Al Green?

a. New York Giants defensive end Michael Strahan

b. San Francisco 49ers cornerback Deion Sanders

c. Green Bay Packers quarterback Brett Favre

d. Kansas City Chiefs tight end Tony Gonzalez

20. Ravens cornerback Chris McAlister once held the NFL record (since broken) for the longest play ever, after he ran back an unsuccessful field goal for 107 yards and a touchdown against the Denver Broncos.

    a. True
    b. False

QUIZ ANSWERS

1. D – Arizona Cardinals

2. A – True

3. A – Ed Reed

4. C – Safety Ed Reed

5. B – Cornerback Corey Ivy

6. A – Linebacker Terrell Suggs

7. B – False

8. C – Guard Mitch Richmond

9. D – Linebacker Zack Orr

10. C – Ray Lewis Fool Moon Bar-B-Que

11. B – Linebacker Ray Lewis

12. A – True

13. D – Linebacker Ray Lewis

14. A – Kansas City Chiefs

15. B – The Arena Football League

16. A – True

17. D – *I Feel Like Going On: Life, Game, and Glory*

18. B – Ballers

19. D – Kansas City Chiefs tight end Tony Gonzalez

20. A – True

DID YOU KNOW?

1. Passes defended is a stat that the NFL began using at the turn of the 21st century. Cornerback Chris McAlister narrowly claimed the lead in that statistic for the Ravens, having 138 in his career, just 3 more than safety Ed Reed.

2. Linebacker Jameel McClain holds the franchise record for most safeties created. He has two in his career, and only six other Ravens players have ever recorded a single safety.

3. Ray Lewis' second season was one for the ages. The Ravens' middle linebacker made 184 tackles that year, which was tops in the NFL, a career-high for Lewis, and (unofficially) the second highest total recorded in league history.

4. Linebacker Terrell Suggs was twice hit with the franchise tag by the Baltimore Ravens, who eventually extended him to a six-year deal in 2009 that was the largest deal ever for a linebacker in the history of the NFL.

5. When Ravens safety Ed Reed picked off a pass, he knew what to do with it. Reed's agility led him to many big returns, and his 1590 interception return yards is the NFL record.

6. Thanks to his prowess on the field and charitable work in the community, Baltimore renamed a street after star

linebacker Ray Lewis. "Ray Lewis Way" became the new name for "North Avenue" in 2010.

7. Former Ravens coach Rex Ryan and safety Ed Reed respected each other so much that Reed briefly went to play for Ryan with the New York Jets. Later, when Ryan was the head coach in Buffalo, he hired Reed to be the assistant defensive backs coach with the Bills.

8. During his rookie year in 2003, Ravens linebacker Terrell Suggs announced his presence in the league immediately. He recorded 12 sacks, which was a Baltimore rookie record. Those sacks included one in each of his first four games.

9. Eric Weddle was known for his versatility and lack of ego. Upon signing with the team as a free agent in 2016, the Ravens asked him to play strong safety and Weddle obliged. The following year, the team signed strong safety Tony Jefferson, so Weddle switched to free safety with no complaints.

10. Defensive back Corey Ivy hurt his kidney in a game against the Broncos in Denver in 2006. The injury was so dangerous that the Ravens had to have their team plane detour to Pittsburgh on the flight home so that Ivy could be treated by a doctor.

CHAPTER 9:

THE TRADING POST

QUIZ TIME!

1. One key trade made by the Baltimore Ravens occurred on August 12, 2011, when the Ravens received wide receiver Lee Evans from the Buffalo Bills. Which player did they give up in return?

    a. Wide receiver John Brown
    b. Defensive tackle Michael McCrary
    c. Cornerback Ron Brooks
    d. Quarterback Tyrod Taylor

2. For four consecutive years in the 2000s, the Ravens traded out of the first round of the NFL draft, acquiring more proven talent in an effort to compete with the Pittsburgh Steelers.

    a. True
    b. False

3. In 2020, the Ravens traded defensive tackle Chris Wormley to the division rival Pittsburgh Steelers. In return, they received a draft pick in which round?

a. 1st round

b. 2nd round

c. 5th round

d. 7th round

4. Which Baltimore quarterback was moved to the Denver Broncos to make way for new QB Lamar Jackson after the Ravens drafted Jackson to be their franchise quarterback?

    a. Joe Flacco

    b. Tony Banks

    c. Tyrod Taylor

    d. Robert Griffin III

5. Before drafting franchise quarterback Joe Flacco in 2000, the Ravens made two trades to move around in the NFL draft. What sort of movements did they make?

    a. Traded down with the Jacksonville Jaguars, then traded up with the Houston Texans

    b. Traded down twice, first with the Kansas City Chiefs, then again with the Atlanta Falcons

    c. Traded up twice, first with the New York Jets, and then with the Cincinnati Bengals

    d. Traded up with the New England Patriots, then traded down with the Seattle Seahawks

6. One of the Ravens' best trades saw them acquire wide receiver Anquan Boldin in exchange for just a 6th-round draft pick. Which team regretted making that deal with Baltimore?

    a. Arizona Cardinals

    b. San Francisco 49ers

80

c. Detroit Lions

d. Buffalo Bills

7. Baltimore has completed more trades with the Cincinnati Bengals than with any other NFL franchise, even though the Bengals are a division rival in the AFC North.

   a. True

   b. False

8. Which player did the Ravens trade to the Philadelphia Eagles so they could move up in the third round of the 2017 NFL draft to select defensive tackle Chris Wormley?

   a. Offensive tackle Marshal Yanda

   b. Wide receiver Alshon Jeffery

   c. Defensive tackle Timmy Jernigan

   d. Running back Boston Scott

9. The Ravens took a chance on which troubled but talented cornerback in 2019, acquiring him from the Los Angeles Rams?

   a. Jalen Ramsey

   b. Marcus Peters

   c. Aqib Talib

   d. Earl Thomas

10. Which running back did the Ravens acquire from the Green Bay Packers in a deal in 2018?

    a. Gus Edwards

    b. Ty Montgomery

    c. Justice Hill

    d. Jamaal Williams

11. In 2020, Baltimore traded tight end Hayden Hurst to the Atlanta Falcons for two draft picks. Who did they select with the draft choice they kept from this deal?

    a. Running back J.K. Dobbins
    b. Defensive back Iman Marshall
    c. Linebacker Matt Judon
    d. Punter Johnny Townshend

12. Baltimore has never in its history completed a trade with the Philadelphia Eagles.

    a. True
    b. False

13. In 2013, the Ravens traded a draft choice for former Indianapolis Colts center A.Q. Shipley. What does the A.Q. in his name stand for?

    a. Anthony Quinton
    b. Albert Quinn
    c. Allan Quay
    d. Andre Quickness

14. The Ravens dealt kicker Kaare Vedvik to the Minnesota Vikings for a 5th-round draft choice in 2019. Which country does Vedvik hail from?

    a. United States of America
    b. France
    c. Senegal
    d. Norway

15. In October 2013, the Ravens acquired left tackle Eugene Monroe from one team and traded left tackle Bryant McKinnie to another team. Which two teams were involved in these deals?

    a. New York Giants and New York Jets
    b. Pittsburgh Steelers and Philadelphia Eagles
    c. San Francisco 49ers and San Diego Chargers
    d. Jacksonville Jaguars and Miami Dolphins

16. In their entire history, the Ravens have never traded away a player who was born in the state of Pennsylvania.

    a. True
    b. False

17. After he didn't work out very well with the Ravens, which team did Baltimore deal linebacker Rolando McClain to?

    a. Washington Redskins
    b. Denver Broncos
    c. Buffalo Bills
    d. Dallas Cowboys

18. Which of the following players was NOT traded to or from Baltimore in 2015 for a 7th-round draft choice?

    a. Guard Nick Easton
    b. Cornerback Willi Davis
    c. Tight end Darren Waller
    d. Wide receiver Chris Givens

19. Which NFC North franchise did Baltimore send long-time nose tackle Haloti Ngata to in 2015?

a. Detroit Lions

b. Green Bay Packers

c. Chicago Bears

d. Minnesota Vikings

20. Baltimore has completed more trades involving quarterbacks than any other position.

a. True

b. False

QUIZ ANSWERS

1. C – Cornerback Ron Brooks
2. B – False
3. C – 5th round
4. A – Joe Flacco
5. A – Traded down with the Jacksonville Jaguars, then traded up with the Houston Texans
6. B – San Francisco 49ers
7. B – False
8. C – Defensive tackle Timmy Jernigan
9. B – Marcus Peters
10. B – Ty Montgomery
11. A – Running back J.K. Dobbins
12. B – False
13. C – Allan Quay
14. D – Norway
15. D – Jacksonville Jaguars and Miami Dolphins
16. B – False
17. D – Dallas Cowboys
18. C – Tight end Darren Waller
19. A – Detroit Lions
20. B – False

DID YOU KNOW?

1. Although trades are rare in the NFL, the Ravens made two deals with the Indianapolis Colts within four months during the 2013 offseason.

2. Baltimore dipped into the bottom of the alphabet in 2014, trading for center Jeremy Zuttah from the Tampa Bay Buccaneers for a 5th-round draft choice.

3. Three years later, Baltimore decided to move on from Zuttah but had to package him with a 6th-round draft choice just to receive a slightly higher 6th-round pick.

4. When the Ravens traded long-time franchise quarterback Joe Flacco to make way for Lamar Jackson, they received mostly salary relief, as Flacco was set to make $18.5 million. Baltimore did receive a 4th-round draft choice, which they used on running back Justice Hill.

5. With the 4th-round draft choice acquired from Detroit in their trade of defensive tackle Haloti Ngata, the Ravens selected talented outside linebacker Za'Darius Smith in 2015.

6. Three offensive linemen were involved in a single swap between Baltimore and Denver in 2015. The Ravens sent center Gino Gradkowski to the Broncos, who also drafted center Connor McGovern with the draft pick they received. Baltimore's draft pick, one round higher, was used on guard Alex Lewis.

7. In 2020, the Ravens loaded up on veterans on their defensive line, acquiring both Calais Campbell from the Jacksonville Jaguars and Yannick Ngakoue from the Minnesota Vikings in trades.

8. Pass catching tight end Dennis Pitta was drafted by the Ravens with one of the three selections they got from Denver in a 2010 trade. Denver used the pick they received from the Ravens to draft quarterback phenom Tim Tebow of the Florida Gators.

9. Tight end Darren Waller was drafted by the Ravens after Baltimore traded up with the Dallas Cowboys to select him in 2014.

10. The Ravens made two separate trades in 2017 involving a center and a 7th-round draft pick. Tony Bergstrom was acquired from Arizona and Luke Bowanko was sent to Jacksonville.

CHAPTER 10:

IN THE DRAFT ROOM

QUIZ TIME!

1. The Ravens have drafted three players who made it to the Hall of Fame and two of those players (linebacker Ray Lewis and safety Ed Reed) went to the same school. Which school did they play for?

    a. Miami Hurricanes
    b. Louisiana State Tigers
    c. Oregon Ducks
    d. Alabama Crimson Tide

2. The Ravens have never held the first overall pick in the NFL draft.

    a. True
    b. False

3. How high did Baltimore select Hall of Fame linebacker Ray Lewis in the 1996 NFL entry draft?

    a. 1st round, 5th overall
    b. 1st round, 26th overall

c. 2nd round, 43rd overall

d. 7th round, 222nd overall

4. Which quarterback did the Ravens select highest in the NFL entry draft, using an 18th overall pick?

a. Kyle Boller

b. Lamar Jackson

c. Robert Griffin III

d. Joe Flacco

5. Who was the first player ever selected by the Ravens in the NFL entry draft?

a. Defensive back Duane Starks

b. Linebacker Peter Boulware

c. Linebacker Ray Lewis

d. Offensive tackle Jonathan Ogden

6. Which player, drafted by the Ravens, went on to score the most touchdowns for another NFL team?

a. Running back Chester Taylor

b. Quarterback Tyrod Taylor

c. Wide receiver Brandon Stokley

d. Quarterback Derek Anderson

7. Baltimore has drafted 10 players who were named first-team All-Pros a single time, including one each in 2016, 2017, and 2018.

a. True

b. False

8. Hall of Fame offensive tackle Jonathan Ogden was selected in which round of the NFL draft?

   a. First round
   b. Second round
   c. Fourth round
   d. Sixth round

9. Fan favorite Torrey Smith was selected in the 2nd round by the Baltimore Ravens in 2011. Which college coach did he play for?

   a. Nick Saban
   b. Butch Davis
   c. Ralph Friedgen
   d. Jim Harbaugh

10. How many years had the Ravens gone without selecting a kicker before taking punter Dave Zastudil during the 4th round in 2002?

    a. Two years
    b. Five years
    c. Six years
    d. Twelve years

11. Which Ravens player was selected highest in the team's 2018 draft class?

    a. Tight end Mark Andrews
    b. Quarterback Lamar Jackson
    c. Offensive tackle Orlando Brown Jr.
    d. Tight end Hayden Hurst

12. The first two draft picks ever made by the Ravens became Pro Football Hall of Fame players.

    a. True
    b. False

13. Which Ravens draftee has accumulated the most career sacks for the franchise, with 139?

    a. Linebacker Adalius Thomas
    b. Linebacker Ray Lewis
    c. Defensive end Pernell McPhee
    d. Linebacker Terrell Suggs

14. In the 1996 NFL draft, Baltimore took Hall of Fame offensive tackle Jonathan Ogden 4th overall. Which one of the following teams did NOT pass on him with a higher pick?

    a. New York Jets
    b. Arizona Cardinals
    c. Jacksonville Jaguars
    d. New York Giants

15. Star linebacker Peter Boulware was drafted by Baltimore 4th overall in the 1997 NFL entry draft. Which Hall of Fame player was selected ahead of him in that draft?

    a. Offensive tackle Orlando Pace of the St. Louis Rams
    b. Offensive tackle Walter Jones of the Seattle Seahawks
    c. Defensive end Jason Taylor of the Miami Dolphins
    d. Tight end Tony Gonzalez of the Kansas City Chiefs

16. The Ravens have held the very last pick in the NFL draft, given the nickname of "Mr. Irrelevant," four times.

    a. True
    b. False

17. Up to and including the 2019 NFL draft and season, Ravens draftees have been selected to how many NFL Pro Bowls?

    a. 62 Pro Bowls
    b. 75 Pro Bowls
    c. 80 Pro Bowls
    d. 97 Pro Bowls

18. Which position has Baltimore traditionally never put a premium on, by never selecting it when they've held a top-10 overall draft pick?

    a. Quarterback
    b. Running back
    c. Wide receiver
    d. Defensive back

19. What is the lowest position in the draft that the Ravens have selected a player who would go on to make the Pro Football Hall of Fame?

    a. 4th pick overall
    b. 26th pick overall
    c. 97th pick overall
    d. 153rd pick overall

20. In 2013, the Ravens had back-to-back selections in the fourth round of the NFL draft, which they used on defensive end John Simon and fullback Kyle Juszczyk.

    a. True
    b. False

QUIZ ANSWERS

1. A – Miami Hurricanes

2. A – True

3. B – 1st round, 26th overall

4. D – Joe Flacco

5. D – Offensive tackle Jonathan Ogden

6. B – Quarterback Tyrod Taylor

7. A – True

8. A – First round

9. C – Ralph Friedgen

10. C – Six years

11. D – Tight end Hayden Hurst

12. A – True

13. D – Linebacker Terrell Suggs

14. D – New York Giants

15. A – Offensive tackle Orlando Pace of the St. Louis Rams

16. B – False

17. D – 97 Pro Bowls

18. A – Quarterback

19. B – 26th pick overall

20. A – True

DID YOU KNOW?

1. Between 1999 and 2013, Baltimore at least one player each year who lasted 100 games in the NFL. The stretch would have lasted from their first year of existence in 1996, except that in 1998 their best choice was defensive back Duane Starks, who lasted "only" 97 games.

2. The Ravens have a penchant for choosing defensive backs high in the draft. Of the franchise's 26 first-round picks, six have been cornerbacks or safeties, the highest of any position group.

3. Offensive tackle Michael Oher came from an impoverished childhood to become a first-round draft pick of the Baltimore Ravens. His story was told in a very popular book, *The Blind Side*, which became a movie that was nominated for the Best Picture Award at the Academy Awards.

4. The Ravens have drafted two players from the University of Maryland. Interestingly, both were wide receivers (Jermaine Lewis in 1996 and Torrey Smith in 2011), and both turned out to be very successful picks for the team.

5. The first Ravens draft pick who went on to play 200 NFL games was linebacker Ray Lewis. Lewis played his entire career with Baltimore, totaling 228 NFL games before his retirement in 2012.

6. Baltimore's top homegrown running back, Jamal Lewis, was drafted by the team in 2000 and finished with over 10,000 rushing yards. In contrast, no wide receiver or tight end drafted by the Ravens even has over 6,000 receiving yards with the club.

7. The largest Ravens draft classes ever were selected in 1997 and 2018, when the team drafted 12 players in each draft. The 1997 class yielded four Pro Bowl selections (all by linebacker Peter Boulware), but the 2018 class has a chance to be even better, as they already have three Pro Bowl selections after just a couple of seasons.

8. When the Houston Texans joined the NFL in 2002, they selected Baltimore wide receiver and kick returner Jermaine Lewis with their 6th choice in the expansion draft. Lewis lasted just one season with the Texans.

9. The Ravens drafted two running backs in the 2008 draft. Seventh-rounder Allen Patrick never played with the team, but second-rounder Ray Rice is atop many of the Ravens rushing leaderboards.

10. The latest pick the Ravens have made in the NFL draft was their 258th overall selection in 2003. They used this on defensive back Antwoine Sanders out of Utah, but Sanders never suited up for the squad.

CHAPTER 11:

ALMA MATERS

QUIZ TIME!

1. Ravens superstar safety Ed Reed referred to his school as "The U." Which school did he attend?

    a. University of Alabama

    b. University of Southern California

    c. University of Miami

    d. Penn State University

2. Because of the rivalry between the two states, the Ravens have never drafted a player from the University of Virginia.

    a. True

    b. False

3. Talented Ravens running back Kyle Juszczyk attended which prestigious Ivy League school?

    a. Yale University

    b. Harvard University

    c. Princeton University

    d. Dartmouth University

4. Stud running back J.K. Dobbins helped "dot the I" at which formidable college football program?

    a. Florida State University
    b. Ohio State University
    c. Michigan State University
    d. University of California

5. Star defender Matt Judon was not as highly scouted as many other players because he attended which little-known school?

    a. Cal-Poly Technical Institute
    b. University of American Samoa
    c. Elon University
    d. Grand Valley State University

6. The current Baltimore squad has three players who have won the Heisman Trophy: quarterbacks Lamar Jackson and Robert Griffin III, and running back Mark Ingram. These Ravens won the Heisman while playing where?

    a. University of California Los Angeles, Texas Tech University, and Boise State University
    b. Florida State University, University of Tennessee, and Temple University
    c. University of Louisville, Baylor University, and University of Alabama
    d. Rutgers University, University of Notre Dame, and Michigan State University

7. During their first decade of existence, the Ravens selected at least one player who attended college in the state of Florida in every single NFL draft.

a. True

b. False

8. With 11 picks each from two schools, the Ravens have drafted more players from which college programs than anywhere else?

    a. University of Alabama Crimson Tide and University of Oklahoma Sooners

    b. University of Miami Hurricanes and University of Florida Gators

    c. University of Notre Dame Fighting Irish and Florida State University Seminoles

    d. University of Nebraska Cornhuskers and Penn State University Nittany Lions

9. In 2008, the Ravens drafted franchise quarterback Joe Flacco, who played for the University of Delaware, in the first round. What was his college team's nickname?

    a. Devil Dogs

    b. Mini Titans

    c. Wild Mastodons

    d. Fightin' Blue Hens

10. In 2018, Baltimore doubled up by selecting two players in the NFL draft from each of the following schools, except for which college?

    a. University of Alabama Crimson Tide

    b. Louisiana State University Tigers

    c. University of Oklahoma Sooners

    d. University of California Los Angeles Bruins

11. Defensive end Za'Darius Smith was drafted by the Ravens in 2015 out of which school that is better known as a basketball powerhouse?

    a. Duke University Blue Devils
    b. University of North Carolina Tar Heels
    c. Georgetown University Hoyas
    d. University of Kentucky Wildcats

12. Defensive end Paul Kruger was a member of two undefeated teams with the University of Utah Utes before being drafted by the Ravens in 2009.

    a. True
    b. False

13. Which future division rival was part of Steve Smith Sr.'s wide receiver group as a Santa Monica Corsair?

    a. Chad Johnson of the Cincinnati Bengals
    b. Hines Ward of the Pittsburgh Steelers
    c. T.J. Houshmandzadeh of the Cincinnati Bengals
    d. Antwaan Randle-El of the Pittsburgh Steelers

14. Current Ravens safety Justin Richards went to which academically elite NCAA institution?

    a. Harvard University
    b. Massachusetts Institute of Technology
    c. Stanford University
    d. University of Pennsylvania

15. After retiring as a player, which former Miami Hurricane and Baltimore Raven returned to the University of Miami to serve as its chief of staff?

a. Linebacker Ray Lewis

b. Cornerback Duane Starks

c. Running back Willis McGahee

d. Safety Ed Reed

16. The only current Baltimore Raven who attended college at the University of Maryland is defensive end Yannick Ngakoue.

    a. True

    b. False

17. Ravens cornerback Marcus Peters came from which college football program?

    a. University of Washington Huskies

    b. Washington State University Cougars

    c. George Washington University Colonials

    d. Eastern Washington University Eagles

18. Four current Ravens attended the University of Texas. Which of the following did NOT play for the Longhorns?

    a. Wide receiver Devin Duvernay

    b. Strong safety Chuck Clark

    c. Kicker Justin Tucker

    d. Guard Patrick Vahe

19. As of 2019, Baltimore had selected players from how many different colleges in the NFL draft?

    a. 53 schools

    b. 68 schools

    c. 81 schools

    d. 96 schools

20. Baltimore has selected more players from foreign countries than players from the state of California.

    a. True
    b. False

QUIZ ANSWERS

1. C – University of Miami

2. B – False

3. B – Harvard University

4. B – Ohio State University

5. D – Grand Valley State University

6. C – University of Louisville, Baylor University, and University of Alabama

7. B – False

8. A – University of Alabama Crimson Tide and University of Oklahoma Sooners

9. D – Fightin' Blue Hens

10. B – Louisiana State University Tigers

11. D – University of Kentucky Wildcats

12. A – True

13. A – Chad Johnson of the Cincinnati Bengals

14. C – Stanford University

15. D – Safety Ed Reed

16. A – True

17. A – University of Washington Huskies

18. B – Strong safety Chuck Clark

19. D – 96 schools

20. B – False

DID YOU KNOW?

1. Baltimore has selected two Arizona State Sun Devils in the first round of the NFL draft: tight end Todd Heap 31st overall in 2001 and linebacker Terrell Suggs 10th overall in 2003. Both picks were massive successes, as Heap and Suggs starred for many years with the Ravens.

2. Morgan Cox has been the long snapper for the Ravens for a decade. Cox is an alumnus of the Tennessee Volunteers, but Baltimore did not spend a draft choice on him coming out of school; they signed him as an undrafted free agent.

3. Three American colleges use the nickname "Ravens," but Baltimore has never selected a player from any of them, so every incoming Ravens rookie has switched nicknames when moving from college to the NFL.

4. In college, Ravens safety Eric Weddle played on both sides of the ball for the Utah Utes. A newspaper columnist wrote "The only people who spend more time on the field than Weddle each Saturday are referees," and an opposing coach once told him "They're cheating you, son; they ought to give you two scholarships."

5. Four current Baltimore players attended the University of Oklahoma, and interestingly, all four play on the offensive side of the ball. Ben Powers (guard) and Orlando Brown Jr (tackle) play on the offensive line, while skill players

Marquise Brown (wide receiver) and Mark Andrews (tight end) were also Sooners.

6. Two current Baltimore offensive players went to Oklahoma State University: running back Justice Hill and wide receiver Dez Bryant. That means that Oklahoma has developed more of the current Baltimore offense than any other state.

7. Among the current Baltimore Ravens team members, North triumphs over South. Linebacker Chris Board went to North Dakota State University, linebacker E.J. Ejiya went to the University of North Texas, and linebacker L.J. Fort went to the University of Northern Iowa. Only wide receiver James Proche II attended Southern Methodist University.

8. Rice University standout tight end Luke Wilson joined the Ravens after taking an unusual athletic path. Wilson was born in Ontario, Canada, and played for the Canadian National Junior Baseball team before being drafted by the Toronto Blue Jays of Major League Baseball. After playing football at Rice, Wilson was also drafted by the Toronto Argonauts of the Canadian Football League.

9. Until 2020, the Ravens had never drafted a player from football powerhouse Louisiana State University. They finally ended this streak by choose linebacker Patrick Queen in the first round.

10. Offensive guard Ben Powers did not get a single scholarship offer from a college program as a high school

senior. Yet, after spending a single year at Butler Community College, he went on to become an All-American first-teamer as a University of Oklahoma Sooner before being drafted by the Ravens.

CHAPTER 12:

COACHES, GMS, & OWNERS

QUIZ TIME!

1. Who served as the Ravens' first general manager?

    a. Art Modell

    b. Eric DeCosta

    c. Bill Parcells

    d. Ozzie Newsome

2. The Baltimore Ravens have employed fewer head coaches in their franchise history than any other team in the NFL.

    a. True

    b. False

3. The Ravens' first head coach, Ted Marchibroda, won how many games during his three seasons with the franchise?

    a. 9 wins

    b. 16 wins

    c. 21 wins

    d. 25 wins

4. Baltimore coach Brian Billick is considered to be a member of which legendary coach's "coaching tree"?

    a. Washington Redskins coach Joe Gibbs

    b. San Francisco 49ers coach Bill Walsh

    c. Miami Dolphins coach Don Shula

    d. Cincinnati Bengals coach Paul Brown

5. Who has owned the Baltimore Ravens for the longest amount of time?

    a. Art Modell

    b. Paul Allen

    c. Steve Bisciotti

    d. Al Lerner

6. Long-time Ravens bench boss John Harbaugh is considered to be a part of which legendary coach's "coaching tree"?

    a. George Halas of the Chicago Bears

    b. Vince Lombardi of the Green Bay Packers

    c. Tom Landry of the Dallas Cowboys

    d. Sid Gillman of the San Diego Chargers

7. Ted Marchibroda coached the Baltimore Colts in the 1970s before coaching the Baltimore Ravens in the 1990s.

    a. True

    b. False

8. Which Baltimore general manager was once an NFL player?

    a. John Lynch

    b. Mike Shanahan

c. Eric DeCosta

d. Ozzie Newsome

9. Which coach led the Ravens to their first Super Bowl championship?

a. Brian Billick

b. Ted Marchibroda

c. Bill Parcells

d. John Harbaugh

10. 10 How many of the Ravens' head coaches have spent their entire NFL coaching career with Baltimore?

a. 0

b. 2

c. 4

d. All of them

11. Who is the Baltimore leader in all-time coaching wins?

a. John Harbaugh

b. Brian Billick

c. Ted Marchibroda

d. It is a tie between John Harbaugh and Brian Billick.

12. Baltimore is the only NFL franchise to have an owner who was once an NFL player.

a. True

b. False

13. How many head coaches have roamed the sidelines for the Ravens in their history?

a. 2

b. 3

c. 7

d. 9

14. Which of the following positions has Ravens leader Ted Marchibroda NOT held during his NFL coaching career?

    a. Head coach

    b. Assistant coach

    c. Offensive coordinator

    d. Defensive coordinator

15. Which general manager has led the Ravens to the most playoff appearances?

    a. Eric DeCosta

    b. Bill Parcells

    c. Ozzie Newsome

    d. Jack Easterby

16. Ravens owner Art Modell once proposed trading franchises with Major League Baseball's Baltimore Orioles owner Peter Angelos as part of a business deal.

    a. True

    b. False

17. Why did future Ravens coach Brian Billick leave the United States Air Force Academy when he was a college student?

    a. He wanted to focus more intently on his future career as a football coach.

b. He found the military discipline and exacting standards too grating.

c. He wanted to attend a school closer to his hometown to help out his ailing mother.

d. He discovered that his size (6'5", 230 pounds) prevented him from being selected as a fighter pilot.

18. How did Steve Bisciotti become the majority owner of the Baltimore Ravens from 2004 to the present?

a. He purchased the team when the previous owner went bankrupt.

b. He inherited the team from his father.

c. As a minority owner, he bought out the shares of Art Modell.

d. He was hired as CEO of the company that owned the team.

19. Which Ravens coach is the only one to have won an award as the league's top coach while behind the bench for Baltimore?

a. Brian Billick

b. Ted Marchibroda

c. John Harbaugh

d. No Ravens coach has ever won this award

20. Baltimore bench boss John Harbaugh began his coaching career with five consecutive trips to the NFL playoffs, culminating in a Super Bowl victory in his fifth year.

a. True

b. False

QUIZ ANSWERS

1. D – Ozzie Newsome

2. A – True

3. B – 16 wins

4. B – San Francisco 49ers coach Bill Walsh

5. C – Steve Bisciotti

6. D – Sid Gillman of the San Diego Chargers

7. A – True

8. C – Ozzie Newsome

9. A – Brian Billick

10. B – 2

11. A – John Harbaugh

12. B – False

13. B – 3

14. D – Defensive coordinator

15. C – Ozzie Newsome

16. B – False

17. D – He discovered that his size (6'5", 230 pounds) prevented him from being selected as a fighter pilot.

18. C – As a minority owner, he bought out the shares of Art Modell.

19. C – John Harbaugh

20. A – True

DID YOU KNOW?

1. The Baltimore Ravens first head coach, Ted Marchibroda had played quarterback for the Pittsburgh Steelers and Chicago Cardinals during the 1950s.

2. In three seasons coaching the Ravens, Ted Marchibroda recorded more tie games (1) than Brian Billick and John Harbaugh combined over 21 seasons (0).

3. When the Ravens were searching for a head coach after firing Brian Billick in 2008, their top choice was Jason Garrett. Garrett chose to remain with the Dallas Cowboys, so the Ravens pivoted to hire John Harbaugh, who has been the leader of the team ever since.

4. After Steve Bisciotti took over as owner of the Ravens, he directed the team to build a top-of-the-line headquarters for practice and training to promote better performance and attract free agents to the club. The facility is known as "The Castle."

5. When Baltimore tabbed Ozzie Newsome to be the franchise's first general manager, it was the first time that an African-American had held that position in the NFL.

6. While some franchises allow their head coaches control over personnel, no one has ever served as both coach AND general manager of the Baltimore Ravens.

7. As college students at Miami (Ohio) University, Ravens coach John Harbaugh shared a room with Brian Pillman,

who would go on to become a famous wrestler called "The Loose Cannon" in the WWE and WCW organizations.

8. The well-traveled Ted Marchibroda coached for four decades in the NFL, spending time with nine different franchises: the Baltimore Ravens, Buffalo Bills, Indianapolis Colts, Baltimore Colts, Philadelphia Eagles, Detroit Lions, Chicago Bears, Los Angeles Rams, and Washington Redskins.

9. Continuity is important in the Ravens' organization. When the team began play in 1996, Ozzie Newsome was the general manager, and Eric DeCosta was a player personnel assistant. Over three decades later, DeCosta is still with the team as the general manager and Newsome is still employed by Baltimore as the executive vice president.

10. After head coach Brian Billick ordered Ravens players not to mention the words "playoffs" or "Super Bowl" during their regular season run toward the team's first championship in 2000, players adopted the term "Festivus" from the hit television show Seinfeld to use for "playoffs" and referred to the Super Bowl as "Festivus Maximus."

CHAPTER 13:

ODDS & ENDS & AWARDS

QUIZ TIME!

1. Which Raven has won the most league MVP trophies while playing for Baltimore?

    a. Linebacker Ray Lewis

    b. Running back Jamal Lewis

    c. Quarterback Lamar Jackson

    d. Quarterback Joe Flacco

2. The first Raven to win any major NFL award was linebacker Peter Boulware, who won the Associated Press NFL Defensive Rookie of the Year Award in 1997.

    a. True

    b. False

3. No Raven has ever won the NFL's Comeback Player of the Year Award while ON the team, but Baltimore did sign wide receiver Steve Smith after he had won the award with the Carolina Panthers. What negative event befell Smith before he returned to the playing field and won the award?

a. He crashed his motorcycle into a lamppost, taking off several layers of skin and separating his shoulder in the fall.

b. He was diagnosed with leukemia and took a season off to treat (and eventually beat) the disease.

c. He suffered two concussions in back-to-back practices and could not return for a year and a half.

d. He broke his leg during a game against the Green Bay Packers.

4. What is Gerry Sandusky's connection to the Baltimore Ravens?

   a. An architect who designed and built M&T Bank Stadium for the Ravens

   b. A beloved groundskeeper who has worked for the Ravens since they joined the NFL in 1996

   c. A player agent who represented linebacker Ray Lewis, safety Ed Reed, and several other Ravens players, mostly from Florida

   d. A long-time radio play-by-play announcer for the Ravens on their home station

5. Three Ravens players have won the NFL's Defensive Player of the Year Award. Which of the following did NOT take home the trophy?

   a. Safety Ed Reed

   b. Defensive tackle Haloti Ngata

   c. Linebacker Ray Lewis

   d. Linebacker Terrell Suggs

6. Who was the first Baltimore Raven to be elected a first-team All-Pro?

    a. Left tackle Jonathan Ogden

    b. Safety Ed Reed

    c. Wide receiver Jermaine Lewis

    d. Running back Jamal Lewis

7. The Baltimore Ravens have the most regular-season wins of any franchise in NFL history.

    a. True

    b. False

8. Only one Raven has ever been named the NFL's offensive player of the year. Who received that honor?

    a. Quarterback Joe Flacco

    b. Quarterback Lamar Jackson

    c. Running back Ray Rice

    d. Running back Jamal Lewis

9. Who is the only Baltimore Ravens assistant to have won the NFL's Assistant Coach of the Year Award while with the team?

    a. Defensive coordinator Rex Ryan

    b. Defensive coordinator Marvin Lewis

    c. Offensive coordinator Greg Roman

    d. Defensive coordinator Don Martindale

10. Who was the Ravens' first Super Bowl MVP?

    a. Quarterback Trent Dilfer

    b. Left tackle Jonathan Ogden

c. Linebacker Ray Lewis

d. Running back Jamal Lewis

11. Which team has defeated the Ravens the most times in the NFL playoffs?

a. Indianapolis Colts

b. Pittsburgh Steelers

c. New England Patriots

d. Tennessee Titans

12. Baltimore is the first NFL team to win the Super Bowl after losing the championship game the previous year.

a. True

b. False

13. Of the 14 Ravens who have been named to three or more Pro Bowls during their careers, how many have played a "skill" position (quarterback, wide receiver, running back, or tight end)?

a. 1

b. 4

c. 6

d. 12

14. How long did it take the Ravens to sell 50,000 season tickets when they went on sale after the team joined the NFL in 1996?

a. 9 hours

b. 5 days

c. 14 days

d. 42 days

15. Who is the only Baltimore Ravens running back to have been selected as a first-team All-Pro more than once?

    a. Ray Rice
    b. Jamal Lewis
    c. Mark Ingram
    d. Vonta Leach

16. Ravens linebacker Ray Lewis was only the second linebacker to win the Super Bowl MVP award.

    a. True
    b. False

17. Tight end Benjamin Watson is the only Baltimore Raven to have been given the Athletes in Action/Bart Starr Award, which he won in 2018. What is this award given out for?

    a. The player who "combines aspects of philanthropy, volunteerism, and charitable involvement in an exemplary fashion"
    b. The player who "refuses to give up, exhibiting maximum effort despite game circumstances that prevent the possibility of a victory"
    c. The player who "contributes his time selflessly to the media, helping to promote the game of football through interaction with the press"
    d. The player who "best exemplifies outstanding character and leadership in the home, on the field, and in the community"

18. In which city is the Baltimore Ravens team headquarters located?

a. Baltimore, Maryland

b. Owings Mills, Maryland

c. Washington, D.C.

d. Philadelphia, Pennsylvania

19. How long was the first field goal ever kicked by a Baltimore Raven (Matt Stover, in 1996)?

a. 18 yards

b. 25 yards

c. 38 yards

d. 51 yards

20. The Ravens are undefeated in Super Bowl games held in a dome.

a. True

b. False

QUIZ ANSWERS

1. C – Quarterback Lamar Jackson

2. A – True

3. D – He broke his leg during a game against the Green Bay Packers.

4. D – A long-time radio play-by-play announcer for the Ravens on their home station

5. B – Defensive tackle Haloti Ngata

6. A – Left tackle Jonathan Ogden

7. B – False

8. D – Running back Jamal Lewis

9. C – Offensive coordinator Greg Roman

10. C – Linebacker Ray Lewis

11. B – Pittsburgh Steelers

12. B – False

13. A – 1

14. C – 14 days

15. D – Vonta Leach

16. A – True

17. D – The player who "best exemplifies outstanding character and leadership in the home, on the field, and in the community"

18. B – Owings Mills, Maryland

19. B – 25 yards

20. A – True

DID YOU KNOW?

1. Only one Raven has ever won the NFL's Walter Payton Man of the Year Award, given for a combination of great play and strong charity or volunteer work in the community. Center Matt Birk was the recipient in 2011.

2. In 2019, the Ravens set a team record and tied the NFL's record by sending 12 players to Hawaii for the Pro Bowl. Six players on offense were chosen, along with four on defense and two special teamers. Only the 1973 Miami Dolphins had previously sent this many players. Two other Ravens were named as alternates, meaning over 25% of the 53-man roster was honored that season.

3. Two Ravens have been named the NFL's Defensive Rookie of the Year. Linebacker Peter Boulware was the first to win, in 1997, and fellow linebacker Terrell Suggs matched him in 2003. No Baltimore player has ever won the NFL's Offensive Rookie of the Year Award.

4. During the 2000 season, the Baltimore defense set the NFL record for fewest points allowed in a 16-game season.

5. The Ravens have won Super Bowl championships in two different venues. Their first title came in 2000 at the Mercedes-Benz Superdome in New Orleans, Louisiana. When they won in 2012, the game was played at Raymond James Stadium in Tampa, Florida.

6. Of the Ravens in the Pro Football Hall of Fame, left tackle Jonathan Ogden was the first to take the field with the Ravens...but it's very close. Linebacker Ray Lewis was in Baltimore's very first game along with Ogden, but the Oakland Raiders kicked off to begin the game, so Ogden took the field before Lewis.

7. Both times the Ravens won the Super Bowl, they scored 34 points against their opponent. In Super Bowl XXXV, they beat the New York Giants 34-7. Super Bowl XLVII was much closer, but the Ravens edged the San Francisco 49ers 34-31.

8. As a young child, Michael McCrary was part of a case decided by the United States Supreme Court (including Justice Byron "Whizzer" White, a former NFL player), when his mother sued a daycare facility that would not accept him due to his race. McCrary was awarded the NFL's Byron "Whizzer" White Man of the Year Award 25 years later.

9. Baltimore running back Jamal Lewis won the 2003 AP NFL Offensive Player of the Year Award after a season in which he rushed for the third-most yards in NFL history and set what was then an NFL record of 295 rushing yards in a single game.

10. Quarterback Lamar Jackson is highly decorated despite his young career. Jackson won the Heisman Trophy while playing for the Louisville Cardinals in 2016 and then was only the second unanimous selection as NFL MVP for the Ravens in 2019.

CONCLUSION

There you have it, an amazing collection of Ravens trivia, information, and statistics at your fingertips! Regardless of how you fared on the quizzes, we hope that you found this book entertaining, enlightening, and educational.

Ideally, you knew many of these details but also learned a good deal more about the history of the Baltimore Ravens, their players, coaches, management, and some of the quirky stories surrounding the team. If you got a little peek into the colorful details that make being a fan so much more enjoyable, then mission accomplished!

The good news is that the trivia doesn't have to stop there! Spread the word. Challenge your fellow Ravens fans to see if they can do any better. Share some of the stories with the next generation to help them become Baltimore supporters, too.

If you are a big enough Ravens fan, consider creating your own quiz with some of the details you know that weren't presented here and then test your friends to see if they can match your knowledge.

The Baltimore Ravens are a storied franchise. They have a long history with multiple periods of success, (and a few that were less than successful). They've had glorious superstars, iconic moments, and hilarious tales, but most of all they have wonderful passionate fans. Thank you for being one of them.